# north country moments

For Bob and Elaine,

Long memories and
some new words
and sketches to carry
them in, with love

From Cliff and Shirley
November, 2006

northern highland state forest — vilas county — sayner — plum lake — frank lake — aurora lake — plum creek — wildwood — starrett lake — st. germain — little st. germain river — boulder junction — alleguash lake — big muskellunge lake — partridge lake — trout river — wild rice lake — alder lake — manitowish river — island lake — manitowish waters — iron county — the flambeau — mercer — turtle river — long lake — valders moraine — northern highland divide — watersmeet — headwaters — gogebic county — montreal river — penokee range — precambrian shield — ironwood — wakefield — lake of the clouds — keweenaw peninsula — lake superior

A Collaboration in Writings and Sketches

# north country moments

By Cliff Wood and Neal Long

Manitowish River Press     Mercer, Wisconsin

NORTH COUNTRY MOMENTS

A collaboration
in Writings and Sketches

Printed in the United States.

Poems and essays by Clifford Wood
Pen-and-ink sketches by Neal D. G. Long
Book design and production by John S. Iwata
Advisory editing by William F. Thompson

Publisher's Cataloging in Publication Data
Wood, Clifford, 1929 –
Long, Neal D. G., 1925 –

North Country Moments: A Collaboration in Writings and Sketches/
Writings by Cliff Wood; sketches by Neal Long
Includes citations, notes and comments
ISBN 0-9656763-2-3 (paperback)
1. Poetry and essays
2. Haiku
3. Wildlife art – Great Lakes Region
4. Natural history observation – Great Lakes Region
5. Nature study – Wisconsin

Library of Congress Catalog Card Number: 00107067

Published by Manitowish River Press
4245 N. Hwy. 47, Mercer, Wisconsin 54547
Phone: (715) 476-2828
FAX: (715) 476-2818
E-mail: manitowish@centurytel.net

To our families and friends

— and all who love the North

From Cliff Wood and Neal Long

*Wood Duck on the St. Germain River*

Grateful acknowledgement is made to the editors of the publications
in which the written selections presented here originally appeared:

American Haibun & Haiga, The Beloit Poetry Journal,
Fox Cry Review, Frogpond, Haiku Quarterly, Modern Haiku,
New Mexico Quarterly, Wisconsin Academy Review,
Wisconsin Poets' Calendar, Wisconsin Review

Detailed acknowledgements and citations appear in the end-pages.

Gratitude is extended also to all who contributed their helpful
observations in the selection and arrangement of sketches and
writings, with special acknowledgement to:

Advisory editor, Bill Thompson,
author and research director with the Wisconsin State Historical Society
and first designated Wisconsin State Historian

Design and production editor, John Iwata,
artist and photographer, and Director of University News & Publications
at the University of Wisconsin-Oshkosh

WRITINGS

# a gift of round stones

# in early snow

# strawberry necklace

# genealogy

SKETCHES

# a gift of round stones

# in early snow

# strawberry necklace

# genealogy

northern highland state forest — vilas county — sayner — plum lake — frank lake — aurora lake — plum creek — wildwood — starrett lake — st. germain — little st. germain river — boulder junction — allequash lake — big muskellunge lake — partridge lake — trout river — wild rice lake — alder lake — manitowish river — island lake — manitowish waters — iron county — the flambeau — mercer — turtle river — long lake — valders moraine — northern highland divide — watersmeet — headwaters — gogebic county — montreal river — penokee range — precambrian shield — ironwood — wakefield — lake of the clouds — keweenaw peninsula — lake superior

# a gift of round stones

## HAIKU MOMENTS

Readers who keep a journal of their Northwoods experiences may find the haiku form of expression an enjoyable and useful one to include. Though short as a single breath in reading, haiku present an opportunity for longer reflection by offering moments of individual human awareness that are stimulated by and drawn into the larger, external world of nature familiar to us all.

Derived from a long and rich tradition in Japan, the haiku as written in North America usually celebrates the seasons of natural life around us, the intuitive rather than analytical modes of our perception, and the small details within our direct observation whose often unexpected combinations and larger implications linger on.

*Canada Geese in Aurora Lake, jumped by an unexpected canoe*

a durable gift of the north country

is the beauty of

ordinary things in their own habitat...

The surviving animals and plants, the undisturbed topography beyond the towns and roadways, the sources of clear water still form a living land independent of our custody. Having extracted the obvious riches of timber and metal and fur, we are just beginning to sense the value of what we have overlooked.

*Woodland Mouse and Wild Strawberries*

Now as visitors in what was long seen as one of the great American frontiers, we find a place that has a way of keeping itself, of receding before us even as we press farther into it. Resilient beneath our adventurous yet more disciplined sports, our moderated hunting and fishing, the living land asserts its own identity.

For individuals, moving deeper into the North Country, becoming closer to it, also allows it to become more a part of ourselves. The seasonal changes and their rigors broaden our sense of time, and a less hurried familiarity with the land begins to emerge. Unnoticed, the forest floor awakens in our eyes. Shorelines and streambeds reveal their intricate communities.

*Eastern Chipmunk will eat from your fingers if you have patience and peanuts*

Perhaps as an even greater gift, the North Woods can gradually lead us from the centers of ourselves to points of perception outside our skin that, in turn, double back to enrich and enlarge the self within. The closer we look into this natural world, the more complex each apparently simple observation can become. Seen on their own terms, the natural features and residents of this land regain their elegance and mystery and depth.

*Loon family and Great Blue Heron on West Plum Lake.*
*These and other loons often seem to 'wave' as they swim by*

## seasoning

Wind shoves the bay ice —
two loons   bill to bill
drift with the melting

Above the frog song
the loon draws a dotted line
around his lake

Autumn sun rises —
in its prism of mist
a young loon still hunts

Gray feather found
and tucked in my hat brim
I know they'll be back

# *standing still*

Rusty dawn
after the maple flame
these oaks

Tamarack gold
slight hiss of needles falling
on the lifting frost

In muted woods
the bluejay's electric arc
a crackling echo

*Blue Jay announces your coming into the woods*

# january thaw

Highland divide
water drawing north and south
beneath the same snow

Tilted sunlight
scattering bright pools
on the cedar swamp

Dark rivulets
mapping hidden channels
in the stream below

Fresh roadcut

through the glacial till —

a gift of round stones

*Small Boat Landing — a peaceful no-motors lake,
one of many so designated since the 1940's*

Just off the bow
a young loon breaches
I hear us both grab for breath

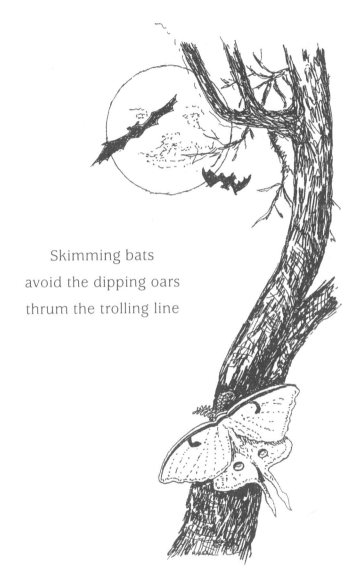

Skimming bats
avoid the dipping oars
thrum the trolling line

*Luna Moth — one of nature's most beautiful night creatures,*
*and one of the many visual rewards of fishing at night*

Small frog cry caught
backward in the snake's mouth —
I watch with two eyes

Third day of rain
the loon tucks new weeds around
her floating nest

Black-tipped ermine
carrying her dark mouse
in a mother's grip

*Ermine with catch,*
*a weasel in its white or winter color phase*

Hummingbird preens
on the smallest branch —
this hidden wingfold

Foggy sunrise
pin cherry at the shoreline
glistening with bees

Evening stream
startled deer leap in a spray
of backlight

*White-Tailed Deer group with Albino Fawn.*
*The Little St. Germain River was home for ten years to an albino doe*
*who had twin brown fawns each spring*

Hatchling turtle
on its way to the lake
swims in my hand

Windfall maples cut
sap rising to a puddle
on each stump

Muskellunge released
his color brightening
in the swirl

*Musky – 'quick release.' This happens often*

Spreading bird seed
on the snow crust —
sweet prairie-dust devils

Two eagles stalking
a pike left for them
wing tips to the snow

*Chickadee — a year-round friend,*
*tame and playful by nature*

Thin deer
in deep marsh snow
breathing short plumes of frost

At the meltline
in spaghnum moss a bear track
crisp with ice

*Black Bear mother and cub.*
*Top of the food chain and symbol of the true woods*
*— and a nuisance around the bird feeder in the spring*

South of the moraine
two kettle ponds turned to bog
in one lifetime

Round stone from northern
stream to southern sand — resting
halfway in my hand

Trumpeter swan
then a boat motor starting
the human day

*Trumpeter Swan on Partridge Lake, an unusual sight and sound*

northern highland state forest — vilas county — sayner — plum lake — frank lake — aurora lake — plum creek — wildwood — starrett lake — st. germain — little st. germain river — boulder junction — allequash lake — big muskellunge lake — partridge lake — trout river — wild rice lake — alder lake — manitowish river — island lake — manitowish waters — iron county — the flambeau — mercer — turtle river — long lake — valders moraine — northern highland divide — watersmeet — headwaters — gogebic county — montreal river — penokee range — precambrian shield — ironwood — wakefield — lake of the clouds — keweenaw peninsula — lake superior

# in early snow

*Bald Eagle and an injured pike that will not go to waste.*
*But a mixed blessing if still attached to a hook and line.*
*Fishermen should always remove hooks*

# the fragility of individual lives

is made more apparent to us in the North Country ...

As humans, our habit is to hold still the events of our experience, to separate them as images and memories and narratives. But here, as we settle into the rhythms of the natural world we have entered, the prevailing sensitivity is to each full moment as it passes and is replaced by the next.

*Musky lunchtime.*
*Mallard chicks are trained to cluster and appear larger from below*

To the animals around us, the controlling process is predation. It is unlikely they see themselves involved, as we do, in dramas and conflicts which imply resolution. They face injury and disease, as we do, and the ultimate predation of time, but with an evenness grown from the cycles of their climate and long adjustments to the pressures of their own evolution.

We can learn from the natural residents of this land to live with their acceptance of brevity. Our sense of proportion is enhanced by insight into their own. Our perspective can broaden to see the constrictions of time and vulnerability as more than predatory — as patrons, also, of the fulfilling moments which contribute the beauty and joy to their existence.

*Red Squirrel — the North Woods' native squirrel
and pine forest chatterer*

A SOLO RENGA
— MOMENTS IN TWO SEASONS
*for Phyllis*

The renga, in haiku tradition, is a
linked form in which each of
thirty-six stanzas proceeds from
the one before and leads to the
one following — though fre-
quently with sudden changes in
focus. Typically, it is composed by
two or more contributors, each re-
sponding to and adding to one
another's imagery. This selection,
while written in one voice, is
speaking for two.

*in early snow*

across the bay
    your cabin in early snow
      each dark log distinct

no rising smoke from the hearth
low landscape of knot and grain ...

no light seeping out
   behind boarded windows
     the furniture waits


trees that still hold their leaves
bent by their sudden load


October moon
   no late loon floats or flies
     this year


a sense of larger movement
now below the surface

your I-V tube
    a dripping icicle
        fluorescent blue


talk in the hospital room
of the lake in summer


melanoma is
    too musical a word
        for snow    dear Sister


a glacier growing in darkness
a crystal inside a stone


the amaryllis
    holds a shadow in its bell
        on your window sill


up North small victories
in January thaw

through a blizzard
　of white corpuscles
　　you face the light

the moon defines our boot prints
to and from your door

the lake still freezing
　pushing against its banks
　　moaning at night

for fishes and for deer
thick ice means safety and feed

　we long for water
　for the slip of a canoe
　　through lilies

we long for a new summer
we long for it for you

*Tiger Swallowtail butterfly*

the nurse is cheerful
   time to go home
      for a while

the plants left behind
their dark-veined leaves

the sun outside
   painful to the eyes
      full and warm

we turn toward it
in spite of what we know

we talk again
   of opening your cabin
      between treatments

the rooms heat easily
too early for the well

pine candles stand
   waiting for the longer day
      to open them


small birds move back with the sun
bush by bush each dawn



   does step carefully
   ready to deliver
      their twins


pike move into the stream beds
under porous ice


April moonscape
   a confusion of tracks
      local migrations


call of circling geese
the shallow ponds are free

full season now
    the loons proclaim their lake
        with tolerance

your color is back as well
quick and certain movements

the first hot muffins
    from your stove   cranberries
        saved from the fall

in momentary silence
we taste this sacrament

outside we know
    your sidelane is crowded
        with forget-me-nots

*The Longwood Boat,*
*sixteen-foot Rhinelander 'wine stem'*

our wooden rowboat
nudging at your dock

A HAIBUN
— ENDLESS MOMENTS
*for Bill Leffin*

The haibun form of this selection
— and of GENEALOGY in the con-
cluding fourth part of the book —
may, again, be of particular inter-
est to readers who keep journals
of the important moments in
their lives. The form offers a prose
narrative, with haiku placed for
emphasis or transition or as rest-
ing points for contemplation...
surrounded by silence.

## from the front

Walking the lake ice
  this late-winter dawn ...

...I cross the bay to check his cabin — 'Eagle's Nest' — on the highest local ridge of a moraine pushed south from Lake Superior over worn-down mountains, former Alps, of the Penokee Range. Avoiding deeper lines in the tiled pattern of shifted and refrozen surface, bulged slightly at the cracks like healing sutures, I can't avoid thinking of the fresh scars and bandages where the doctors have just seen and agreed not to pull back the malignant hand of tissue that has him by the neck.

From down here I note that the cabin rests against its settled snowbanks, gradually emerging on the southern slope.

*under its dark tarp*
*a cord of split firewood*
*drawing the light*

For forty years and more, he has been a healer and a giver for the rest of us, taking wounds on our behalf. As a young medic, a volunteer in Korea — he told me once — he was trapped at the front for days and endless nights. In his foxhole, grown familiar with the pistol he had not expected to need, he waited every dusk for the Turks to come from behind, foraging their way across enemy lines. First there was the scent of garlic; then the touch of the curved knife blade at his throat; then the left hand over his shoulder and down inside his shirt, feeling for the identifying tags that labeled him to live.

He made it back from the front knowing that what may have seemed to be ritual was not. Knowing how to carry his shrapnel wounds lightly enough that they would not be a bother to us. Still ahead — as artist, teacher, dean of our faculties — he had other lives to lead.

*fresh rubs last fall*
*blazing an old deer trail*
*from the deep marsh*

Then suddenly, five years ago — when an aneurysm mush-roomed inside him like a vagrant, slow-motion bullet — he was back in the foxhole of himself. Centered in a snow-white room, he could hear the doctors talking to one another, yet could not speak out to them, give them the vital direction they, and we, would need as they felt and felt his chest. Months later, when he returned to us — more or less seeming to have been here all along — we somehow believed his war was finally over.

And now this. This waiting for another return. This stern, exhausting faith in the strength of a man.

*a thick walking stick*
*from beneath the eagle's tree*
*to use today*

I turn toward home in my own footprints, feel the warmth of the sun on the back of my collar. The winds, too, are beginning their shift to the southeast. Maybe word will come today at the post office box or over the thin rural phone line.

*Timber Wolf — a black wolf at late dusk on Starrett Lake Road.*
*A rare encounter with the true North*

Last night on the news, old images of a new generation of fit and confident youngsters mustering below the DMZ. Watching them poised on the edges of their private uncertainties, I summoned what prayers I could that they like he will come away from that front, come back here with those of us less chosen to be ravaged by our dangerous lives.

*at the outlet stream*
*platelets of shoreline ice*
*melting from below*

SECULAR PRAYER
— A MOMENT DELAYED
*for Kim and Fred*

One value of written response is that it gives us the opportunity to say to each other, later on, something that our emotions told us at a heightened moment was true but which our comprehension and reflection were not yet adequate to express. This selection was composed several weeks following a rural Wisconsin church service for a victim of Sudden Infant Death Syndrome.

*Woodcock and Fiddlehead fern.*
*The 'timber doodler' at rest*

# tulip child

His month of life will grow around him still.
This small boy, uncurling like a fern,
legs barely straight, had just begun to learn
the touch of sunlight when that sudden frost
which slows the spring stayed long enough to fill
his shallow breathing, close him to return
the long-familiar posture he had lost.

Last fall they planted tulips as a charm,
in thanks for gifts to come from earth and flesh,
to bring new color every year in fresh
remembrance of the pressure then asleep,
and now still lingering along the arm —
for them a double garden they must keep.

As for the rest of us, each bulb or root
we hold will be less dormant, be more real,
and when we press it to the soil will feel
firm and stirring as a newborn foot.

northern highland state forest — vilas
county — sayner — plum lake — frank
lake — aurora lake — plum creek —
wildwood — starrett lake — st. germain
— little st. germain river — boulder
junction — allequash lake — big
muskellunge lake — partridge lake —
trout river — wild rice lake — alder
lake — manitowish river — island lake
— manitowish waters — iron county —
the flambeau — mercer — turtle river
— long lake — valders moraine —
northern highland divide — watersmeet
— headwaters — gogebic county
— montreal river — penokee range —
precambrian shield — ironwood
— wakefield — lake of the clouds —
keweenaw peninsula — lake superior

strawberry necklace

MOMENTS IN PLACE

There is a bit of Thoreau in most Americans, a desire to slow down, to explore the edges of our natural environments in order to know better the spirit of the places where we live and the dimensions of our more personal relationships to them.

One such place, a home base for five years — visited, returned to, then lived in year 'round by the couple in this section of the book — was a lake-edge log cabin in Iron County, Wisconsin. This originally home-made cottage was located almost directly atop the Northern Highland Continental Divide, on one of the northernmost lakes to drain south. A rainfall or snowmelt there could go either way. If one could place a message in a molecule, it would eventually reach either the Gulf of Mexico or the North Atlantic. Perhaps there is a bit of that north/south polarity in all of us as well.

*as a couple living year 'round
in a remote lake cabin,*

the routine actions of daily life soon settle
into a greater significance ...

Splitting, stacking, drying wood for the fireplace is no longer just an enjoyable autumn exercise. It is a matter of keeping your mate alive. Long before the saw and axe, on casual summer walks or snowshoe treks the year before, the eye has almost instinctively marked likely trees to cull. In deepest cold, trips to town for more gunny sacks of seed for birds and corn for the clustered deer take on the purposeful satisfaction of real work.

*Raccoon — the masked bandit that eats anything and everything*

Animals drawn in winter to the only lighted cabin remain unafraid in the abundance and movement of other seasons. Even the largest leave their tracks on the open dew. The shared austerity of Northwoods life brings animals and plants and people into the same clearings — dependent upon each others' generosity and restraint.

The many moments of quiet isolation draw a man and a woman closer together as well. While fishing a still bay or rowing the shoreline at evening, their silence becomes a language. Watching life below and at the water's edge becomes a metaphor for their own intimacy. And sounds from the deep woods beyond bring new harmonies to a mutual audience of two.

*Cottontail Rabbit — one of two species in the North Woods,*
*the other being the snowshoe or varying hare, both active year-round*

Even leaving the cabin, boarding it up, is a preparation to return. All absence, however long, seems temporary. And all their experiences of other lands, brought home, fit in.

INTIMATE MOMENTS

Though they are not properly haiku or sequences, the ten 'Valentines' in this section found their language in the same seductive, syllabic music of that form, and also — more distantly — in an ancient Japanese love-poem tradition known as 'waka.'

Likewise, many readers may prefer to buy the 'blank cards' and write their own intimate messages. Those fortunate enough may have the talent to do their own sketches as well.

Strawberry   necklace
I cup her chin in my hand
soft hummingbird throat

*Ruby-Throated Hummingbird — nature's jewels,*
*their very existence wondrous and incomprehensible*

## since when

You in a sundress
driving barefoot to the lake
and climbing the dunes

your first sidelong glance
fixed the hunter in his place
prickling on your trail

You found the safe spot
in whatever scape or course
and let him catch up


How he purrs inside
as I tend our cabin fire
memorizing spring
to sense your quickening pulse
your arrow still in the air

*Pileated Woodpecker — the North Woods woodpecker,*
*the size of a crow, guided by acute hearing*
*to insect movement in dead or infested trees*

# *two weeks*

*February, North —*

Outside the cabin
four snowshoes lean together
  against the woodpile
Tracks pass a balsam and pine
growing as a single tree


Breath frost on your scarf
melts like firegeese in the grate,
  coats steam on a chair
Holding our mugs with both hands
we sip re-heated coffee


Wind pries at the logs
You wear my thick flannel shirt
  in the sleeping bag
Tomorrow it will carry
with me the gift of your warmth

*February, South —*

    Walking the white beach
I follow your slight footprints,
    carry your sandals
Shorebirds run ahead of us,
inspect each receding wave

    Watching the sunset
we hear our voices distant
    as the whorl of shells
I speak a wish in your ear
as the sand sinks beneath us

    Moonlight on our sheet
defines the shades of your tan
    and my darker hand
All night we lie almost still,
open to the shifting air

# landing

Framed in the window
at thirty-three thousand feet
the peninsula
barely rises from the gulf —
a shimmering gift of ice
still trapped in the north
withholding its tendril streams
from the parent sea.

Unwound by the airplane wing
all day a scroll of rivers
has wrinkled southward
peeling away its tribute
from places we've lived —
from granite Wisconsin hills
and loam soils of the Midwest.

We've followed the earth
past its alluvial plain
to slowly touch down
on an intimate new sand
growing from the oldest grains.

## return trip

I slip without words
into your new element
  a warm pool at night


  Neighboring palm fronds
scatter a rising moonlight
  to catch your whiteness


  I follow a glint
of earring   the wind-chime sound
  of ripple on tile


  Then suddenly close
I sense your touch drawing me
  to our youth once more
to your deep  Geneva lake,
upstream to my river source

White coffee mugs

her tongue a summer wren

behind her lips

*Wren — will live in a 'house,'*
*though usually nests in low bushes.*
*Not shy of people*
*but not thought of as tame*

# *cabin dawn*

Your French crystal frog
(out of his box since Christmas)
   is in full display

   at this dawn window
(the sun inching north each day)
   where you last left him,

   a prince in waiting
(mimicking his countrymen)
   leaning after you,

   a curved fleshy glow
(as I interpret for him)
   showing readiness
to yield more light when he can
attract your transforming touch

# *in concert*

Knitting a sweater
for a child,  you concentrate,
    smiling to yourself
as ducklings start to emerge
from their white and yellow spools,
    your fingers slowly
tending them to a blue field.


    I pretend to read
each time you glance up over
your  'sexy librarian'
    glasses, sensing when
you are probably counting.


    But I am thinking
about those fingers — touching
them across a cafe booth
    or on silent drives
down backwoods Wisconsin roads,
    on awakening
or at evening in the cup
of their most intimate braille.

In the concert hall
last month,  we heard the grand dame
    De Larrocha bring
Mendelssohn back to a life
more vibrant than even he
    could have expected —
such power in her small hands.


    At the slow movement —
the baton more visible
for its stillness,  the cellists
    floating on their bows —
an image came drifting back:
    a Venetian shop,
you lift a mask by its wand
and wed me to the moment.

# *waiting*

Our first sign of spring:
waist-high snowpack subsiding
over summer trails.

We keep to the road,
noon sun just clearing the trees
drawn to dark objects.

Red osier dogwood,
redder, we say, more finches
yellow at their throats.

Back in the cabin
I slide off our steaming coats
and your high black boots,
press your cold toes to my cheek,
white roots waiting for the thaw.

*Goldfinch pair — stays all winter in a brown color phase,*
*the brilliant gold returning in the spring. Easily attracted to thistle seeds*

# caring enough

I stand a lone man
in a close row of women
picking valentines
for you, granddaughters, seeking
images to match my own:

Your bright round faces
budding from their snowsuit pods,
so like your mothers

Posing with a toe
dipped into a new dance step
or cold-water lake

Holding up your fish
before we put it back in
to keep on growing

The sly private smile
after just saying something
you knew was clever

Waving back to us
as you leave on your ride home,
goodbye hugs still warm.

I turn to the touch
at my elbow — a picture
perfect valentine
this moment when you are all
your grandmother to me.

northern highland state forest — vilas county — sayner — plum lake — frank lake — aurora lake — plum creek — wildwood — starrett lake — st. germain — little st. germain river — boulder junction — allequash lake — big muskellunge lake — partridge lake — trout river — wild rice lake — alder lake — manitowish river — island lake — manitowish waters — iron county — the flambeau — mercer — turtle river — long lake — valders moraine — northern highland divide — watersmeet — headwaters — gogebic county — montreal river — penokee range — precambrian shield — ironwood — wakefield — lake of the clouds — keweenaw peninsula — lake superior

# genealogy

*Musky in weeds — a large female, over 50 inches,*
*that for many years patrolled her territory around*
*and under the dock at the Long family resort on Plum Lake*

## the way north

is like an ever narrowing trail into the mountains ...

The roads and byways, following the curvature of the globe, bend away from the sun, gain distance from the grasslands below.  Each hundred miles feels like a thousand feet in altitude.  The air thins and clears.  In the hills and valleys more spires of fir and tamarack arise.  Yet the steady, ascending path, as if in memory of high ranges gone, is drawn down tight against the bedrock, drawn back in time.

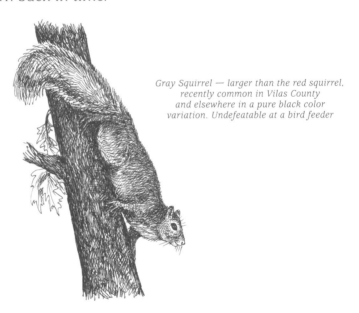

*Gray Squirrel — larger than the red squirrel, recently common in Vilas County and elsewhere in a pure black color variation. Undefeatable at a bird feeder*

We come here from different places at different times in our lives, but most from lowland cities.  We sense that passing days are in our favor here.  The ancient land and natural world growing upon it seem welcoming — as if the species we now are had never wholly left.

In their innocence of time, children can make of this land whatever their imaginations wish, construct from its unfamiliar freshness whole new realms to occupy. In a few years they will sense the many levels of their own experience with the land — the impact of its human histories, the slow flow and ebb of its changing ecology, and the even slower sense of suspension in a glacial drama everywhere evident. Later, if observant and receptive enough, they may gain the gift of insight into the deep past of the land, to the birth and formation of the very earth on which they stand.

*Ruffed Grouse all puffed up strutting and displaying, often heard 'drumming' in the spring. Locally called 'partridge'*

For many, the road North is also a journey to the interior of the self. We push upstream like spawning fish, upwind like returning geese, pulled on by a sense of origin. We look down into deeper, clearer water. We stand at the edge of a vast marsh to get our bearings. The magnetic pole may wander, but North is always a bright compass point in the soul.

MOMENTS IN TIME

A life of moving closer to the
North Country leads one gradu-
ally to feel the constant undertow
in its currents of time — from the
surface strata of passing mo-
ments in nature and thin accumu-
lations of human experience,
through a jumble of glacial oblit-
erations and rearrangements, to
the sudden exposures of vast
depths of bedrock below.

THIS SANDPILE
*for Jan and Cindy*

One of the enduring paradoxes of
growing up is the wish to seize
the fleeting moment, to hold it
still. But the ability to do so that
children have at play comes from
their very sense of timelessness.
Adults observing such innocence,
as in this selection, can no longer
separate those moments from
their own deepening awareness
of 'time's arrow.'

# *this sandpile*

bound in a worn-out tractor tire
  is a continent
adrift in the Midwestern air —
  an experiment
in deserts whose mirages show
a parallel to no Arabian scroll,
  whose pinecone camels will endure
whatever myths the six-year-olds conjure.


  Nomadic neighbor
boys wink and scuff until the girls'
  delicate labor
toward pastry crumbles to sugar swirls.
Then, with a whoop and a pail of water, like drakes
  they splay the sand.  The eldest makes
his order to gather stones;  the word's a sign:
  let it be tanks and a battle-line.


A fable later the caravan's
  abandoned the mound
to the baby's crab-fast, intrusive hands
  and the nosing hound
that soon erode a castle's eminence.
No matter; no drama here has permanence:
  the shifting dunes of a sand-pile plot
  bury kings next to camels well as not.

*to*
*Willis, Butterfield*
*and McKenzie*

Is human time part of nature, or above nature? Three young theologians and a 'fisherman' once toyed with this unspoken question for a few hours. Then, ready to go home, one of them asked, flat-out: "What is your ontological position?" Now, there is something to muse about for a few more years on the way North — especially on Sunday mornings.

# letter to three ministers

The scene was Kansas: you'll recall the walk

we took one Sunday afternoon, along

an old escarpment of the Flint Hills, past

Jacob's Creek and down the windward valley

between two deserted farms.  It was my turn

to play the parson, having earned the right

that morning by catching a good bass at the willow

pool and cooking him for lunch on the bank

You came out after church to look around,
and what we saw was scripture — of a sort.
The aspect of that world was an immediate
fact, but looking made it metaphor:
trees growing bent from the prevailing wind,
last winter's coyotes hanging on the fences
by the road,  the run of a wild dog pack
winding just below the crest of the hills
that told us why we need not look for rabbits
or for deer.  The frost had begun to loosen
in the rock shelves, enough to start the large
springs up again.  We knelt by one the size
of an arm to listen to the water moving
deep inside with a sound like a distant choir
or the ambiguous plaint of an old god trapped.

*Largemouth Bass
— one of the true game fish*

*Red Fox with partridge prey*

Farther on we found the usual sign
of fox — a slash, a stain, and a mat of feathers.
But the real luck was the owl pellet.
Under the bare rafters of the broken
farmhouse I cut it open to show the mouse
inside, digested, disarticulate
but whole, its teeth still in the jawbone; a seeming
comfort in its immortality
becoming stone.   Then, just like that, we saw
him — dark, heavy, near enough
to have been watching — glide from a sycamore tree,
follow the slope of the ground; and he was gone.

I frequently recall that walk on Sunday
mornings, on my way to fish or hunt,
driving out of this Wisconsin town
in a clamor of bells, past new washed cars along
the curbs;  think of you three on a mound
overlooking ninety miles of uninterrupted
West,  and think of what you must have seen —
a trinity, a promise, or a threat.

*Great Horned Owl — nearly the size of an eagle.*
*Source of the hoot in the night*

# vilas winter

Such sudden cold gives back the land its own
integrity — a simple fact of stone.

The brevity of summer seems a lie,
an opulence arranged to falsify

the other hints that are here, but are not seen
in other seasons:  here in the cold green

shapes of pike, in the official words
that next year we may expect fewer birds;

in the well-known habits of the bears, and in
the spring ice-shove on the lakes:  a thin

reflection of a distant glacial snow
still pressing downward — patient, slow —

or an iceberg that obscures its old intent
by separating from its continent.

So, too, this parent rock, Precambrian shield,
where the planet sticks out through a shallow field

allowing the streams to deepen its bright scars,
proclaims no kinship with the cooling stars.

The hunter goes home early, may forget
his own and his land's great tendency, but let

him come in winter;  he sees it then
such as it was and will be again.

...With a tip of the hunting cap
to Bob Brismaster for several
deep-winter snowshoe treks at
Statehouse Lake north of Mani-
towish Waters and in the sand
country of central Wisconsin at
35 below zero. The first real
awareness of glacial time – par-
ticularly of its almost ominous
contemporary presence – does
not come from reading, however
exciting that may be in itself

DEEP TIME

Just north of the Valders Moraine
in Iron County, Wisconsin – along
U.S. Route 2, between Wakefield
and Marenisco, Michigan – parts
of the deepest history of our
planet lie exposed for us to view,
more than three billion years
later. The 'greenstone' referred to
in this haibun, and which out-
crops two miles east of Wake-
field, is a basaltic lava from that
formative time which was most
recently metamorphosed as the
core of the Penokee range, one
and a half billion years ago.

*Beavers — nature's most industrious mammal,
constructing their house*

# why do so many come to feel at home here,

wherever they were born — return to the Northern
Highland over whole lifetimes to confirm the growing
notion that it seems the place they really came from?

# genealogy

Partly it is a matter of learning how to look at this beguiling scene, with its green glaze and ornament of bright waters, its high dome sloping north to the Superior basin and edge of the world-encircling boreal forest.     To see beneath its human past — mushroom rings defining where the shorn stumps of virgin hemlock and pine have finally subsided, lake bottoms strewn with lost logs, the char of native campgrounds or their portages once narrow and unobtrusive as deer trails — and to follow the land's own genealogy.

*wandering north*
*in deep woods, guided by moss*
*and shadows*

Everywhere we live on a layered earth whose deep history is read in canyons and roadcuts, mine shafts and the sleeves of wells. Yet here, for a few counties, we walk at once on the surfaces of two lands only — the original and the most recent, present together for a moment in time. Barely out from under the latest pulse of ice, both striated bedrock and the thin till that spills around and over it are gifts of the glaciers — revealing the oldest in its place, while bringing in fresh fragments of a wider world.

This youthful landscape, its rivers clear and marshes full, growing but a few inches of soil in a mere eight-thousand years, lives on sand and minerals and the slight nourishment of its own decay. Here fans of pebbles and boulder trains imported from the Canadian shield have hardly begun to weather in the frost and sun that will release their grains into the northbound streams and toward the sea again. For now, their mica flakes glint in the shadows of trees or along the shores of wind-riffled bays like eyes in a minnow school.

> *inlet stream —*
> *its marly delta turbid*
> *with small lives*

To this bedrock province, the low hills and ledges rebounding slowly from the departed ice are the roots of its remnant mountain range — many times uplifted, folded, worn down to a mounded plain, buried in sediment only to be exhumed, raised, and worn down again.  Yet the land retains its shape of arch and syncline, the persistent warp of the world — the core of an alpine chain and a rift that sank into the weight of its own lava flows.   Clouds on the horizon, swelling as they rise inland from the great lake, often seem to trace the vanished outline of those peaks, mimic the inner turbulence that drove them to such height.

The first life here, at this base of the rock-bound earth, some say was born of iron and water. And it holds that character still in its colors and tenacious forms.  With the first iron precipitate and the first sulphurous bacteria, all life and all of us inside it drew from those same stony elements that dissolved, compacted and combined in sea water and air to ignite all chemistries to come.

The aboriginal wisdom was to sense they were a people who had emerged directly from the earth.

Placing a hand on the oldest greenstone outcrop, feeling its warmth as it draws the sun, feeling the sun pass through the hand on its axis into the darker rock, is to feel the youth of a world still growing, to feel very close to having come home.

*surprisingly light —*
*this rock shard carrying*
*three billion years*

From the high escarpment, Lake Superior is indeed an inland sea, an ocean of sweet water as the voyageurs called it, but viewed or imagined from a greater distance it is the widest spot in a river seeking its way, wearing its current route downward while probing still at its former escape to the south. A recent presence in the greater basin, this undrained watershed has begun to leave behind the signs of its diminishing scale — wave-carved shorelines and beaches deserted high above the water, river valleys stranded aloft as crevices in the Precambrian ridge, channels now for snowmelt and wind.

How far we have come with this floating continent that once appeared so stable, but whose vast array of pasts and futures and our origins within now seem as moments in a longer memory — in the earth's own balance of brevities. Perhaps this vista, so undulant and forested to us, will drain and fill and dry away to a desiccated flat — or perhaps will be the stage of another mile-high ice front pushing before it centuries of snow and permafrost to overspread this deep-rock highland, renewing it with drift and boulders for another time.

*pathway down —*
*feeling the pressure of stone*
*beneath the mulch*

northern highland state forest — vilas county — sayner — plum lake — frank lake — aurora lake — plum creek — wildwood — starrett lake — st. germain — little st. germain river — boulder junction — allequash lake — big muskellunge lake — partridge lake — trout river — wild rice lake — alder lake — manitowish river — island lake — manitowish waters — iron county — the flambeau — mercer — turtle river — long lake — valders moraine — northern highland divide — watersmeet — headwaters — gogebic county — montreal river — penokee range — precambrian shield — ironwood — wakefield — lake of the clouds — keweenaw peninsula — lake superior

*Loon calling — the sound of the real North,*
*from here to Alaska. Though migratory in winter*
*as far as Florida, a loon pair will return to the same northern lake*
*just after ice-out in the spring*

## ACKNOWLEDGEMENTS

Publications and Editors

AHH     American Haibun & Haiga
        Editor, Jim Kacian

BPJ      The Beloit Poetry Journal
        Editor, Marion K. Stocking

FOX      Fox Cry Review
        Editors: Donald Hrubesky; Laurel Mills

FP        Frogpond
        Editors: Elizabeth Searle Lamb; Sylvia Forges-Ryan;
               Kenneth C. Leibman

HQ       Haiku Quarterly
        Editor, Linda E. Valentine

MHA     Midwest Haiku Anthology
        Editors, Randy M. Brooks and Lee Gurga

MH       Modern Haiku
        Editor, Robert Spiess

NMQ     New Mexico Quarterly
        Editor, Roland Dickey

WAR     Wisconsin Academy Review
        Editor, Faith B. Miracle

WPC     Wisconsin Poets' Calendar
        Editors: Helen Fahrbach; Iefke Goldberger; Laurel Mills

WR       Wisconsin Review
        General editor, Douglas Flaherty; Poetry editor, Diana Madison

WRA     Wisconsin Review Anthology
        General editor, Douglas Flaherty; Poetry editor, Allyson Bennett

## CITATIONS

Some selections have been revised or altered from their original appearance in typography, capitalization, titling, and page layout where necessary to provide a consistent format.

Seasoning (WPC '91, ed., HF) — Standing Still (MH 23:1 '92, untitled) — January Thaw (MH 25:2 '94) — Fresh roadcut... (HQ 2:4 '90-91) — Just off the bow... (FP 13:4 '90, ed., ESL) — Skimming bats... (FP 13:4 '90, ed.,ESL) — Small frog cry caught... (MH 21:1 '90) — Third day of rain... (FP 14:3 '91, ed., SF-R) — Black-tipped ermine... (MH 22:2 '91 and MHA '92) — Hummingbird preens... (MH 21:1 '90) — Foggy sunrise... (MH 23:3 '92) — Evening stream... (FP 13:4 '90, ed., ESL) — Hatchling turtle... (MH 24:3 '93) — Windfall maples cut... (MH 23:3 '92) — Muskellunge released... (MH, 21:3 '90) — Spreading bird seed... (MH 24:2 '93) — Two eagles stalking... (MH 24:2 '93) — Thin deer... (MH 20:3 '89) — At the meltline... (MH 23:2 '92, revision) — South of the moraine... (FP 18:3 '95, ed., KCL) — Round stone from northern... (FOX v 15 '89, ed., DH, excerpt) — Trumpeter swan... (FP 18:3 '95, ed., KCL)

In Early Snow (MH 22:1 '91) — From The Front (MH 26:1 '95) — Tulip Child (BPJ 38:2 '87-88)

Strawberry necklace... (MH 25:1 '94) — Since When (WPC '95, ed., LM, entitled 'Valentine') — Two Weeks (WR 25:2,3 '91, entitled 'Double Valentine') — Landing (WAR 42:3 '96) — Return Trip (WAR 42:3 '96) — White coffee mugs... (MH 21:2 '90 and MHA '92) — Cabin Dawn (not previously published) — In Concert (FOX v 25, Fall '99, ed. LM, entitled "Your Fingers') — Waiting (WPC '94, ed., IG, entitled 'Valentine') — Caring Enough (FOX v 18 '92, ed., DH, entitled 'Valentine')

This Sandpile (NMQ 27:1,2 '57, revision) — Letter To Three Ministers (NMQ 35:1 '65 and WRA 21:2,3 '87) — Vilas Winter (NMQ 35:1 '65 and WRA 21:2,3 '87) — Genealogy (AHH, v 1, Spring, 2000)

North Country Moments display type was composed in Pepita MT, the text is Usherwood Book and the illustration notes are set in Usherwood Book Italic. The cover is 10pt Carolina CIS printed with four-color process + Pantone 4635 (brown) + UV coating; text sheet is 70# Cougar Opaque printed with Pantone 4635. The book was produced on an Apple Macintosh G4 using Adobe PageMaker 6.5 and Adobe Photoshop 5.5. Printing and binding by Castle-Pierce Printing Co., Oshkosh, Wisconsin.

# order form

**Telephone Orders:** (715) 476-2828  Have your Visa or MasterCard ready.

**Fax Orders:** Fax this order form to: (715) 476-2818

**E-mail Orders:** manitowish@centurytel.net

**Postal Orders:** Mail this order form to: Manitowish River Press, 4245 N. Hwy. 47, Mercer, WI 54547

Check the following books that you wish to order. You may return any book for a full refund, no questions asked, as long as it is in like-new saleable condition.

| Title | Price | Quantity | Total |
|---|---|---|---|
| **North Country Moments**<br>by Cliff Wood and Neal Long | $14.95 | _____ | _____ |
| **A Northwoods Companion:**<br>**Spring and Summer**<br>by John Bates | $14.95 | _____ | _____ |
| **A Northwoods Companion:**<br>**Fall and Winter**<br>by John Bates | $14.95 | _____ | _____ |

**Sales Tax:** Please add 5.5% for books shipped to Wisconsin addresses _____

**Shipping:** *Book rate:* $2.50 for the first book, $1 for each additional. *Priority mail:* $4 first book, $2 each additional. _____

| TOTAL | |
|---|---|

Name _____

Address _____

City _____ State _____ ZIP _____

Phone (_____) _____ Fax (_____) _____

E-mail address _____

Payment:
  ❑ Check   Credit Card: ❑ Visa ❑ MasterCard

Card No. _____ Exp. date _____

Signature _____

# order form